Searchlight BOOKS™

World Traveler

D1092425

A Look at

Ukraine

Matt Doeden

Lerner Publications ◆ Minneapolis

Content consultant: Marcia Amidon Lusted

Lerner Publications Company
An imprint of Lerner Publishing Group, Inc.
241 First Avenue North
Minneapolis, MN 55401 USA

For reading levels and more information, look up this title at www.lernerbooks.com.

Main body text set in Adrianna Regular.
Typeface provided by Chank.

Map illustration on page 29 by Laura K. Westlund.

Editor: Brianna Kaiser **Photo Editor:** Annie Zheng

Library of Congress Cataloging-in-Publication Data

Names: Doeden, Matt, author.
Title: A look at Ukraine / Matt Doeden.
Description: Minneapolis : Lerner Publications , [2024] | Series: Searchlight books - world traveler | Includes bibliographical references and index. | Audience: Ages 8–11 | Audience: Grades 4–6 | Summary: "Learn all about Ukraine, a country in eastern Europe. In this book, readers will explore Ukraine's history, government, and geography. Then they will learn about the religions, languages, and more found in the country"— Provided by publisher.
Identifiers: LCCN 2022038324 (print) | LCCN 2022038325 (ebook) | ISBN 9781728491653 (library binding) | ISBN 9798765603796 (paperback) | ISBN 9798765600795 (ebook)
Subjects: LCSH: Ukraine—Juvenile literature.
Classification: LCC DK508.515 .D64 2024 (print) | LCC DK508.515 (ebook) | DDC 947.7— dc23/eng/20220823

LC record available at https://lccn.loc.gov/2022038324
LC ebook record available at https://lccn.loc.gov/2022038325

Manufactured in the United States of America
2-1009745-51114-5/31/2023

Table of Contents

Chapter 1

GEOGRAPHY AND CLIMATE

Ukraine covers 233,032 square miles (603,550 sq. km) in eastern Europe. Moldova, Romania, Hungary, Slovakia, and Poland border it to the west. Belarus forms its northwestern border. Russia lies to the east and northeast. The Black Sea and the Sea of Azov form Ukraine's southern border. The Crimean Peninsula lies to the south.

Most of Ukraine lies on the East European Plain. The land is mostly flat. Its rich soil makes it great for agriculture. Ukraine is sometimes called the breadbasket of Europe because it grows so much grain.

Ukraine has two main highland areas. The Carpathian Mountains rise in the far western part of the country. The nation's highest point, Mount Hoverla, is part of this range. Its peak rises 6,762 feet (2,061 m) above sea level. The Crimean Mountains lie in Crimea.

Fields of wheat grow on the plains of Ukraine.

Rivers and Lakes

More than twenty thousand rivers flow across Ukraine.
Its longest is the Dnieper. It flows 1,368 miles (2,201 km)
through western Russia, Belarus, and Ukraine and
empties into the Black Sea. Many of Ukraine's biggest
cities, including the capital Kyiv, lie along its banks.
Other major rivers in Ukraine include the Southern Bug
(sometimes spelled Buh), Dniester, and Donets.

The Dnieper is one
of thousands of
rivers in Ukraine.

AN AERIAL VIEW OF LAKE KUHURLUI AND LAKE YALPUH

Ukraine has more than three thousand lakes. Lake Yalpuh is the nation's largest natural lake. It lies in southern Ukraine, near the borders of Moldova and Romania. It's a shallow lake, covering about 58 square miles (150 sq. km). Larger reservoirs, created by people, include the Kremenchuk and the Kakhovka.

Country Highlight:
Carpathian National Nature Park

Nature lovers enjoy the country's tallest mountain range at the Carpathian National Nature Park. The park is home to glacial lakes, birch and pine tree forests, and peat bogs. Many animals are also in the park, including brown bears, wolves, otters, and lynx. Another highlight is the Zhenetskyi Huk, a waterfall that drops 50 feet (15 m).

Climate

Most of Ukraine has a temperate climate. It has four seasons. Summers are warm and wet. Winters are cold and drier, although snow is common across most of the country. The far southern part of Ukraine has a warmer climate, with snowfall being less common. In the summer, thunderstorms rumble across Ukraine's plains. Tornadoes are uncommon in most of Europe. But Ukraine can have them.

Two people row a canoe on a snowy day in Kyiv, Ukraine.

Chapter 2

HISTORY AND GOVERNMENT

People have been living in Ukraine for more than thirty-two thousand years. Many groups settled in the region. They include the Gravettian, Cimmerian, and Sarmatian peoples. Other cultures came and went, especially along the shores of the Black Sea. The Greek, Roman, and Byzantine Empires all held land in Ukraine.

A PART OF A HARNESS MADE BY CIMMERIANS

New Powers

By around 300 CE, the Antes settled in southern Ukraine. They are the ancestors of many modern Ukrainians. Their lives were centered on agriculture. They used iron plows to work the fertile soil. The Antes were also warriors. They built large armies to protect their lands from foreign invaders.

The red portion of the map represents the Soviet Union.

In the 800s, the first East Slavic state, Kievan Rus, formed. It included parts of present-day Ukraine, Belarus, and Russia. The city of Kyiv was its capital. Kievan Rus was a powerful state for more than 250 years. It began to weaken in the 1000s and collapsed during the Mongol invasion in the 1200s.

New powers rose and fell in Ukraine over the next several hundred years. Poland and Russia both claimed parts of Ukraine. In 1657, a civil war called the Ruin broke out. It lasted thirty years.

Over time, Ukraine fell under Russia's control. In 1922, fifteen countries including Russia and Ukraine formed the Soviet Union.

Independence and War

Life in the Soviet Union was often harsh. Its economy struggled. Its people faced hardships. Things worsened for Ukraine in 1986. The Chernobyl Nuclear Power Plant exploded. The disaster spread dangerous radioactive waste. Parts of northern Ukraine became unsafe to live in.

The Soviet Union collapsed in 1991. Ukraine became an independent country. Its people voted Leonid Kravchuk as its first president.

After it exploded on April 26, the Chernobyl Nuclear Power Plant spread radioactive waste.

In the 2000s, Ukraine formed stronger ties with western Europe. Its relationship with Russia became tense. But in November 2013, President Viktor Yanukovych, who was supported by Russia, chose not to sign an agreement to strengthen Ukraine's relationship with the European Union. Ukrainians protested in Kyiv's

Maidan square. The Euromaidan protests grew and became known as the Revolution of Dignity.

Leonid Kravchuk was the president of Ukraine from 1991 to 1994.

People in Irpin, Ukraine, evacuate as the Russian military invades on March 9, 2022.

Ukraine's government began arresting and assaulting the protesters. Some protesters were killed. Then, in February 2014, Russia invaded and took over Crimea—a part of southern Ukraine. But the protesters had a victory that month by forcing Yanukovych out of the country.

In 2022, the Russian military invaded Ukraine. Russian leaders believed that Ukraine's ties to the West were growing too strong. They saw that as a threat and wanted greater control of the country. Russia also thought of Crimea as part of Russia.

Millions of people fled. Global support for Ukraine and President Volodymyr Zelensky came quickly. Countries sent food, weapons, and other supplies. Many cut trade with Russia. Many, including the United States, feared starting a larger world war. Ukraine's people were left to fight for themselves. The war took a terrible toll on the country. Cities were destroyed. Countless citizens and soldiers were killed. The war continues, but Ukrainians continue to stand up against Russia. Zelensky has praised the strength of Ukrainians.

President Volodymyr Zelensky speaks during a press conference in August 2022.

24 серпня 2022 року
Київ

Country Highlight:
Podilski Tovtry National Nature Park

History, natural beauty, and wildlife are on display at **Podilski Tovtry National Nature Park** in southwestern Ukraine. The park features scenic river views, rolling hills, and ancient ruins. Wildlife thrives in the park. Long-eared owls perch in trees, while great egrets gather near the water. Bats live in the park's many caves. The park sits on an ancient seabed. Fossils of the creatures that once lived there can be found.

Government

Ukraine has a semi-presidential republic. Its people elect most of their leaders, including the president. They elected Zelensky president in 2019. The president serves as head of state and appoints a prime minister to serve as head of government. Together, they lead the nation's executive branch.

The legislative branch, the Verkhovna Rada, passes laws. Citizens elect about half of its members. Political parties appoint the other half. Laws require the parties to keep a balance of men and women as members.

The judicial branch enforces the laws. The Supreme Court of Ukraine is the highest court in the land.

The Verkhovna Rada building is in Kyiv.

Chapter 3

CULTURE AND PEOPLE

Ukraine's people share a culture rich in art, music, food, and history. About 78 percent of the country's people identify ethnically as Ukrainian. Around 17 percent are Russian. The remaining 5 percent of people come from a range of ethnic groups, including Belarusian, Moldovan, Crimean Tatar, Bulgarian, Hungarian, Romanian, Polish, and Jewish.

Religion

About 56 percent of Ukraine's people are Christians. Most of them are Ukrainian Orthodox. This faith was established more than one thousand years ago. Smaller numbers of Ukraine's people are Catholic or Protestant.

About 1 percent of people in Ukraine are Muslims. They follow the Islamic faith. Another half of a percent are Jewish. More than 40 percent of Ukraine's people do not follow any religion.

The Saint Sophia Cathedral in Kyiv was built during the eleventh century.

Language and Writing

Ukrainian is Ukraine's official language. About 68 percent of people speak it as their main language. Ukrainian is a Slavic language. It is related to Russian, Polish, and other languages spoken across the region.

About 30 percent of Ukrainians speak Russian. It was the official language when the country was part of the Soviet Union. Smaller numbers of Ukraine's people speak Crimean Tatar, Moldovan, Romanian, and Hungarian.

Ukrainian and other Slavic languages are written in the Cyrillic alphabet. It includes thirty-three letters.

A BOWL OF BORSCHT

▼

Food and Art

Ukraine's cuisine draws from thousands of years of tradition. Food staples in the country include grains such as wheat and rye, pork, fish, and root vegetables such as beets.

Ukraine's national dish is borscht. This soup takes its sour flavor and color from red beets. Varenyky are dumplings stuffed with meat, cheese, potatoes, and more. Stuffed cabbage, sweet babka bread, and sweet cakes called tortes are popular dishes.

Country Highlight:
Kamianets-Podilskyi Castle

A visit to the city of Kamianets-Podilskyi in western Ukraine is like stepping into a fairy tale. The stone castle at the heart of the city is more than eight hundred years old. It overlooks the scenic Smotrych River canyon. Cobbled streets, hot-air balloon rides over the city, and the chance to practice archery on the castle's bridge are just a few things people enjoy at this site.

Ukraine has a distinct style of art and crafts. Christian themes are a big part of much of the country's visual art. Craftspeople create wood carvings, ceramics, and highly detailed Easter eggs called pysanky. Ukrainian folk music often features traditional instruments such as the bandura—a stringed instrument similar to a lute.

A man plays the bandura in Ukraine in 2018.

Chapter 4

DAILY LIFE

About 70 percent of Ukrainians live in urban areas. Kyiv is the capital and largest city. Other major cities include Kharkiv, Odesa, and Dnipro.

Almost 68 percent of Ukrainians work in the service industry. Banking, communications, food service, and tourism are a few of the nation's biggest employers. About 26 percent work in industry. They build machinery such as aircraft, produce electricity, and mine coal and natural gas. About 6 percent of people work in agriculture. They grow grains such as wheat and corn, both major exports of Ukraine.

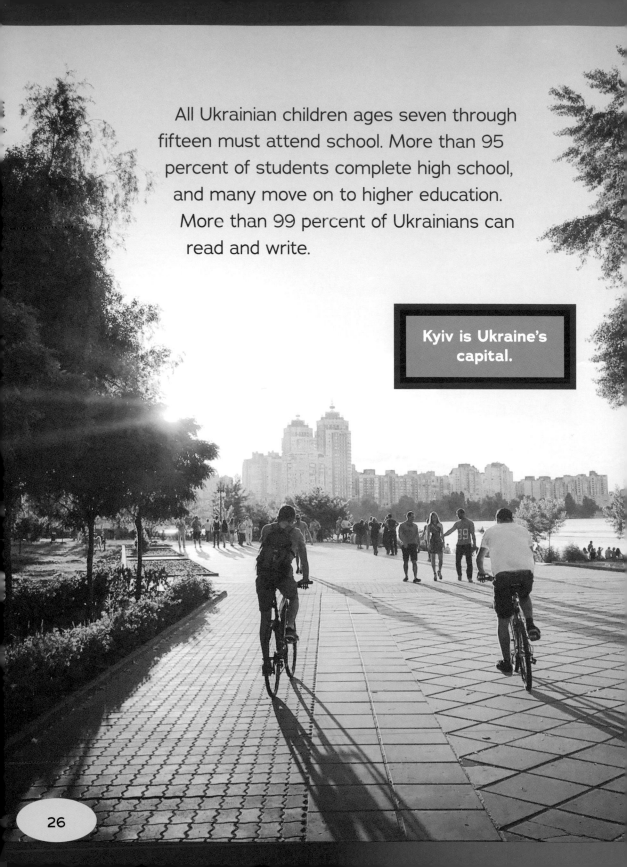

All Ukrainian children ages seven through fifteen must attend school. More than 95 percent of students complete high school, and many move on to higher education. More than 99 percent of Ukrainians can read and write.

Kyiv is Ukraine's capital.

Country Highlight:
Centaurs International Horse Stunt Festival

Horses have played a big role in the history of Ukraine. Its people celebrate all things horses at the annual Centaurs International Horse Stunt Festival in Kyiv. Horses and their riders wow audiences with tricks, jumps, and competitions. Visitors can even saddle up and take a ride of their own.

Future Challenges

The 2022 war with Russia has left Ukraine with an uncertain future. Millions of people have fled the nation. Many others have died. Cities lie in ruins. When the war ends, the Ukrainian people face huge challenges to rebuild their country. Tensions with Russia are likely to last for generations.

Ukraine also faces challenges from climate change. The rise of global temperatures has caused changes in weather patterns. That could threaten Ukraine's crops. Meanwhile, rising sea levels could flood towns and cities along the coast of the Black Sea.

The challenges are big. But Ukrainians have shown that they will fight for a brighter future. They hope to rebuild the country back stronger and better than ever.

#StandWithUKRAINE

STOP PUTIN NOW

On August 24, 2022, Ukraine's Independence Day, people hold a demonstration to protest the Russian invasion.

Map and Key Facts

POLAND

BELARUS

RUSSIA

SLOVAKIA

UKRAINE ★ Kyiv

Kharkiv •

**Kamianets-
Podilskyi
Castle**

Dnieper River

Dniester River

Donets River

Southern Bug River

Dnipro

HUNGARY

MOLDOVA

**Carpathian
National
Nature Park**

Odesa

ROMANIA

Sea of
Azov

Lake
Yalpuh

CRIMEA

RUSSIA

BLACK SEA

ARCTIC OCEAN

NORTH
AMERICA

EUROPE

Ukraine

ASIA

ATLANTIC
OCEAN

AFRICA

PACIFIC
OCEAN

PACIFIC
OCEAN

SOUTH
AMERICA

INDIAN
OCEAN

AUSTRALIA

SOUTHERN OCEAN

Miles
0   50   100
0   80   160
Kilometers

N

★ Capital city
◎ Landmark
⋀⋀ Mountains

**Flag of
Ukraine**

- **Continent: Europe**
- **Capital city: Kyiv**
- **Population: 43,528,136**
- **Languages: Ukrainian, Russian,
  Crimean Tatar, and several others**

Glossary

ancestor: a person, such as a great-grandparent, from whom one is descended

civil war: a battle for power among different groups within a country

fertile: able to grow crops easily

invade: to enter a foreign land with a military

radioactive: containing materials that decay and give off dangerous radiation

reservoir: a large lake, often artificial, used as a water supply

Slavic: a language family that includes Ukrainian and Russian

temperate: a climate with four distinct seasons: spring, summer, fall, and winter

Learn More

Bolte, Mari. *Volodymyr Zelensky: Heroic Leader of Ukraine*. Minneapolis: Lerner Publications, 2023.

Kids World Travel Guide: Ukraine
https://www.kids-world-travel-guide.com/ukraine-for-kids.html

Klepeis, Alicia Z. *Ukraine*. Minneapolis: Bellwether Media, 2021.

Kortemeier, Todd. *Chernobyl*. Minneapolis: Core Library, 2020.

National Geographic Kids: Ukraine
https://kids.nationalgeographic.com/geography/countries/article/ukraine

Time for Kids: War in Ukraine
https://www.timeforkids.com/g56/war-in-ukraine-2/?rl=en-880

Index

Photo Acknowledgments

Image credits: Yuriy_Kulik/iStock/Getty Images, p. 5; Santiago Urquijo/Moment/Getty Images, p. 6; Andriy Nekrasov/Shutterstock, p. 7; Misha Reme/Wikimedia Commons (CC BY-SA 4.0), p. 8; Cavan Images/Getty Images, p. 9; Dea/A. Dagli Orti/De Agostini/Getty Images, p. 11; Opka/Shutterstock, p. 12; KP/Alamy Stock Photo, p. 13; Georges DeKeerle/Sygma/Getty Images, p. 14; Drop of Light/Shutterstock, p. 15; Genya Savilov/AFP/Getty Images, p. 16; Kateryna Polyanska/Wikimedia Commons (CC BY-SA 3.0), p. 17; blurAZ/Shutterstock, p. 18; Farion_O/Shutterstock, p. 20; Roman.S-Photographer/Shutterstock, p. 21; Timolina/Shutterstock, p. 22; Taras Verkhovynets/Shutterstock, p. 23; Havoc/Shutterstock, p. 24; Elena Kozlova/EyeEm/Getty Images, p. 26; The Len/Shutterstock, p. 27; NurPhoto/Getty Images, p. 28.

Cover: Oleg Totskyi/Shutterstock.